Everyday Miracles: Recognizing God's Presence

By: Brian Adams

Welcome to "Everyday Miracles: Recognizing God's Presence"!

Thank you for joining us on this journey of discovery. Together, we'll explore how to recognize God's presence in the ordinary moments of our lives. This study is about cultivating awareness, finding purpose, and experiencing the deep joy that comes from seeing God in every detail of our daily walk. Your willingness to take part is a blessing, and we're grateful to share this journey with you.

If you enjoy this study, we invite you to check out our other Bible studies as well. Each one is designed to help you grow deeper in your faith and see God's hand at work in different aspects of your life. Thank you again for being a part of this journey!

www.amazon.com/author/adams.brian1

Thank you,

Brian Adams

Small Group Guidelines

Review these guidelines at the start of each session.

1. **Confidentiality:** What is shared in the group stays in the group. Respect each other's privacy to foster a safe and trusting environment.

2. **Respect for All Voices:** Encourage everyone to participate and share their thoughts. Respect differing opinions and listen without interrupting.

3. **Punctuality:** Arrive on time and stay for the entire session. Value each other's time and commitment to the group.

4. **Preparation:** Come prepared having read the assigned scripture or materials. This shows respect for the group's time and enhances the discussion.

5. **Prayerful Support:** Begin and end each session with prayer. Offer to pray for one another, respecting individual prayer requests and needs.

6. **Stay on Topic:** Keep discussions focused on the designated scripture or topic. This ensures that conversations are productive and beneficial for everyone's spiritual growth.

7. **Encourage Growth:** Challenge each other to apply biblical teachings to daily life, but do so with kindness and encouragement.

8. **No Judgement:** Foster an atmosphere where questions and doubts can be expressed without fear of judgment. Remember, we are all on a journey of faith and learning.

9. **Conflict Resolution:** Address disagreements or conflicts within the group promptly and biblically, always aiming for reconciliation and unity.

10. **Celebrate Milestones:** Acknowledge the group's progress and individual growth. Celebrate milestones and encourage one another in your spiritual journeys.

By adhering to these guidelines, your Bible study group can create a nurturing and enriching environment that promotes spiritual growth and strong community bonds.

Session 1: Opening Our Eyes to God's Presence

Opening Prayer

"Dear Heavenly Father, thank You for gathering us here today to draw closer to You. We come with open hearts, ready to learn, to be challenged, and to grow. Help us to become more aware of Your presence in our daily lives, especially in the small, often-overlooked moments. Guide us to see the beauty in the ordinary and to recognize Your hand in every detail. Open our eyes, Lord, so that we may see You working all around us. We invite Your Holy Spirit into this time and ask that You reveal Yourself to each of us in a unique way. In Jesus' name, we pray, Amen."

Session Introduction

Today's session is all about beginning our journey of seeing God in the everyday moments. Often, we look for God in big, miraculous events but forget that He is present in the small, seemingly mundane aspects of our lives as well. This session invites us to slow down and develop a habit of attentiveness, allowing us to see and appreciate God's presence in unexpected ways. As we dive into this study, let's be intentional about opening our eyes and hearts to the subtle and beautiful ways God is at work around us every day.

Scripture Reading and Reflections

Jeremiah 29:13

"You will seek me and find me when you seek me with all your heart."

Reflection:

This verse reminds us that finding God is not a passive act but requires our active seeking. It's about approaching our days with intentionality, looking for God in every moment, and bringing our whole heart into that pursuit. This scripture encourages us to take responsibility for our spiritual awareness and to search for God with a heart that longs to see Him, even in the smallest details.

Psalm 121:1-2

"I lift up my eyes to the mountains—where does my help come from? My help comes from the Lord, the Maker of heaven and earth."

Reflection:

This passage encourages us to look beyond ourselves and our immediate circumstances and recognize God's creation and presence. It is a reminder that God is our constant help, present in every aspect of life, from the mountains to the mundane. It calls us to trust in His continual presence and assistance.

Matthew 6:25-26

"Therefore I tell you, do not worry about your life, what you will eat or drink; or about your body, what you will wear. Is not life more than food, and the body more than clothes? Look at the birds of the air; they do not sow or reap or store away in barns, and yet your heavenly Father feeds them. Are you not much more valuable than they?"

Reflection:

Here, Jesus teaches us about God's intimate care, even in the smallest needs. Just as He cares for the birds, He cares deeply for each of us. This passage encourages us to trust that God is present and attentive, even in the smallest concerns, and to release our worries to Him.

Psalm 46:10

"He says, 'Be still, and know that I am God; I will be exalted among the nations, I will be exalted in the earth.'"

Reflection:

In a busy world, this verse reminds us that stillness allows us to become aware of God's presence. By taking moments to pause and be still, we open ourselves to see and experience God in ways we might miss in the rush of life. This stillness is an act of faith, acknowledging that God is at work and inviting Him to reveal Himself to us.

Discussion Points

What are some ways that we can intentionally look for God's presence in our everyday lives?

Why do you think it's often easier to see God in big moments rather than in small, ordinary ones?

Reflecting on Jeremiah 29:13, how can we seek God with all our hearts in daily life?

Psalm 121 speaks of lifting our eyes to God for help. How can changing our focus help us become more aware of God's work in our lives?

Jesus encourages us not to worry in Matthew 6:25-26. How might worrying less open our hearts to see God's care and provision more clearly?

What does "being still" (Psalm 46:10) mean to you, and how does it help you experience God's presence?

Can you recall a recent experience where you felt God's presence in a small way? What made that moment special?

What changes in mindset or habit could help you notice God's presence more in your daily life?

Session Recap

In today's session, we explored the importance of opening our eyes and hearts to God's presence in everyday life. We reflected on scriptures that call us to seek God actively, to trust in His daily provision, and to embrace stillness as a pathway to knowing Him. As we go through this week, let's be intentional in our pursuit of God, recognizing that He is often found in the quiet, ordinary moments. May we carry a renewed awareness that He is with us in all things, waiting for us to see His hand at work.

Closing Prayer

"Lord, thank You for the time we have shared together in Your presence. We ask that You continue to open our hearts and minds to see You at work in our lives every day. Help us to become aware of the beauty in the small and simple things and to understand that You are with us in every moment. May we grow in gratitude and attentiveness, always seeking You with open hearts. Guide us to release any worry and to rest in the knowledge that You are our constant help and provider. In Jesus' name, we pray, Amen."

Homework

Scripture Memory Verse:

Jeremiah 29:13 - *"You will seek me and find me when you seek me with all your heart."*

Daily Journal Reflection Topic:

Spend a few moments each day reflecting on one small way you sensed God's presence.

Write down a sentence or two describing how it made you feel and what you think God was trying to show you in that moment.

This session encourages a deeper awareness of God's subtle presence and prepares participants for a journey of spiritual attentiveness.

Notes:

Session 2: Finding God in Nature

Opening Prayer

"Lord God, Creator of all things, we come before You with gratitude and awe. Thank You for the beauty and wonder of the world You have made, for every flower, tree, and mountain that declares Your glory. Open our eyes to see Your handiwork in creation, and may it remind us of Your presence, Your power, and Your care for us. Guide us in this time together as we explore how Your creation reflects Your character and love. Let our hearts be attuned to Your Spirit, and help us draw closer to You through our connection with the natural world. In Jesus' name, we pray, Amen."

Session Introduction

Today, we'll focus on seeing God through His creation. Nature is filled with signs of God's creativity, power, and provision. Often, we take the beauty around us for granted or don't pause to reflect on what it says about God. This session will encourage us to look more closely at the natural world and see it as a reflection of the Creator. By cultivating this awareness, we can deepen our relationship with God and recognize His presence in the world around us.

Reflection on Previous Week

As we look back on last week's session, let's think about what it was like to open our eyes to God's presence in everyday life. Were there moments where you became aware of His hand in small details? Did you experience any unexpected encounters with His presence? Remember, each week is a building block, helping us grow in attentiveness to God's work around us.

Reflection on Homework

Last week's homework encouraged us to keep a daily journal, noting one small way we sensed God's presence. Did you find this exercise challenging, or did it help you become more aware of God's presence? This practice is foundational, helping us build a habit of noticing God in everyday moments. Share any insights or moments that stood out to you with the group.

Scripture Reading and Reflections

Psalm 19:1-4

"The heavens declare the glory of God; the skies proclaim the work of his hands. Day after day they pour forth speech; night after night they reveal knowledge. They have no speech, they use no words; no sound is heard from them. Yet their voice goes out into all the earth, their words to the ends of the world."

Reflection:

This psalm reminds us that creation itself proclaims God's glory. Even without words, the sky, stars, and sun testify to the Creator's majesty. Every time we look up, we're witnessing a divine message of beauty and power, a reminder that God is present and actively involved in sustaining all things.

Romans 1:20

"For since the creation of the world God's invisible qualities—his eternal power and divine nature—have been clearly seen, being understood from what has been made, so that people are without excuse."

Reflection:

Paul tells us that God's nature and power are visible through creation. When we observe the intricate design and order in the world around us, we gain a glimpse of God's wisdom and character. This verse calls us to see nature as a revelation of who God is, encouraging us to look more closely at the world He created.

Job 12:7-10

"But ask the animals, and they will teach you, or the birds in the sky, and they will tell you; or speak to the earth, and it will teach you, or let the fish in the sea inform you. Which of all these does not know that the hand of the Lord has done this? In his hand is the life of every creature and the breath of all mankind."

Reflection: Job points to nature—animals, birds, and the earth itself—as teachers that reveal God's hand. This passage invites us to learn from creation and see it as a testimony of God's provision, power, and care. Each creature and natural element is a living testimony of God's sustaining presence.

Genesis 1:31

"God saw all that he had made, and it was very good. And there was evening, and there was morning—the sixth day."

Reflection: In this verse, God looks at all He created and declares it "very good." This statement of satisfaction reflects the intentionality and love with which He crafted each part of creation. By recognizing the goodness in creation, we can appreciate God's joy in what He made and understand that He sees value and purpose in every aspect of His creation.

Discussion Points

How does Psalm 19:1-4 change your perspective on observing the world around you?

When you see a beautiful landscape or natural scene, do you feel more connected to God? Why or why not?

Romans 1:20 speaks of God's qualities being visible through creation. What specific aspects of nature reveal God's character to you?

In Job 12, we're encouraged to learn from animals and the earth. What are some lessons we can learn from observing animals or nature?

Genesis 1:31 reminds us that God found creation "very good." How does this impact the way we view nature's value and our responsibility toward it?

How can spending time in nature influence our awareness of God's presence?

What small parts of nature, like flowers or birds, help you connect with God, and why?

How can we incorporate moments of reflection on nature into our daily routines to keep us mindful of God's presence?

Session Recap

In today's session, we explored the idea that God reveals Himself through creation. The natural world, from vast landscapes to small creatures, serves as a reflection of God's beauty, power, and care. By paying attention to these aspects of nature, we can develop a deeper awareness of God's presence. This week, let's challenge ourselves to see the world as God's canvas, painted with reminders of His love and majesty.

Closing Prayer

"Lord, thank You for this time to reflect on the beauty of Your creation. We are in awe of the way nature reveals Your power, wisdom, and love. Help us to see You in every detail of the world around us, from the smallest flower to the tallest mountain. Teach us to appreciate Your handiwork and to recognize that each part of creation is a reflection of Your character. As we go through this week, may our hearts and minds remain open to seeing You in the beauty of the natural world. In Jesus' name, Amen."

Homework

Scripture Memory Verse:

Psalm 19:1 - *"The heavens declare the glory of God; the skies proclaim the work of his hands."*

Daily Journal Reflection Topic:

Take a few minutes each day to write about one part of nature that reminds you of God.

Reflect on what it reveals to you about God's character—His creativity, power, beauty, or love.

This session encourages participants to find God in the beauty of creation and to reflect on how the natural world reveals His attributes.

Notes:

Session 3: God's Voice in Quiet Moments

Opening Prayer

"Lord, we come before You in awe of Your gentle presence and the peace You offer us. Thank You for being a God who speaks to us, not always in loud or dramatic ways, but often in the quietness and stillness of our hearts. Help us to become still and attentive to Your voice. Remove distractions from our minds, quiet the noise in our souls, and prepare us to hear You. Guide us in this time of reflection so that we may learn to recognize and cherish Your voice. In Jesus' name, we pray, Amen."

Session Introduction

This session invites us to explore the beauty of stillness and the ways God speaks to us in quiet moments. In today's busy world, we're often surrounded by noise—both external and internal. But God's voice is often a gentle whisper, heard most clearly when we are still and focused. Learning to quiet our minds and listen for God requires intention and patience, but it opens us to profound spiritual encounters. Let's take time today to discover how we can hear God more clearly in the silence and let His peace fill our hearts.

Reflection on Previous Week

Reflecting on last week, we discussed seeing God in nature. Were you able to find God's fingerprints in creation around you? Did spending time in nature reveal new aspects of God's character? Feel free to share any insights or moments where you felt especially connected to God through His creation.

Reflection on Homework

The homework last week was to journal about a part of nature that reminds you of God. How did this exercise impact your daily perspective? Were there any revelations about God's power, creativity, or care that struck you? These reflections help us remain mindful and continually aware of God's presence.

Scripture Reading and Reflections

1 Kings 19:11-13

"The Lord said, 'Go out and stand on the mountain in the presence of the Lord, for the Lord is about to pass by.' Then a great and powerful wind tore the mountains apart and shattered the rocks before the Lord, but the Lord was not in the wind. After the wind there was an earthquake, but the Lord was not in the earthquake. After the earthquake came a fire, but the Lord was not in the fire. And after the fire came a gentle whisper."

Reflection:

God's voice was not in the powerful, dramatic forces but in the gentle whisper. This passage reminds us that God often speaks to us in quiet, subtle ways. To hear Him, we need to seek silence and stillness. This story encourages us to set aside time for quietness, trusting that God's voice can be found in gentle whispers.

Psalm 46:10

"He says, 'Be still, and know that I am God; I will be exalted among the nations, I will be exalted in the earth.'"

Reflection:

Being still is an invitation to stop, rest, and recognize God's sovereignty. It's in this stillness that we become aware of His presence and are reminded of who He is. This verse challenges us to release control, quiet our busy minds, and allow God to speak into our lives without distraction.

Isaiah 30:15

"This is what the Sovereign Lord, the Holy One of Israel, says: 'In repentance and rest is your salvation, in quietness and trust is your strength, but you would have none of it.'"

Reflection:

This verse highlights the strength we gain from quietness and trust. God invites us to find rest and renewal in Him, not through busyness but through repentance, quietness, and trust. This is a reminder that true spiritual strength comes from aligning ourselves with God in stillness.

Mark 1:35

"Very early in the morning, while it was still dark, Jesus got up, left the house and went off to a solitary place, where he prayed."

Reflection:

Jesus Himself sought quiet moments to connect with the Father. Despite His busy ministry, Jesus prioritized solitude and prayer, modeling the importance of setting aside time for stillness and communion with God. This verse encourages us to follow His example and seek out quiet, uninterrupted moments to connect with God.

Discussion Points

In 1 Kings 19, why do you think God chose to speak to Elijah in a gentle whisper rather than through powerful signs?

What are some common distractions or noises in our lives that prevent us from hearing God?

How does Psalm 46:10 encourage us to "be still" in practical ways?

In what ways can we make room for more stillness and quiet in our daily routines?

Isaiah 30:15 speaks about strength in quietness and trust. What might "quietness" look like in your life, and how can it strengthen your faith?

How does Jesus' example in Mark 1:35 inspire us to seek solitude and prayer?

When you take time to be still and listen, do you feel closer to God? Why or why not?

What practical steps can we take to hear God's gentle voice in our daily lives?

Session Recap

Today, we focused on hearing God's voice in quiet moments. Through scripture, we learned that God often speaks to us in subtle ways, requiring us to be still, patient, and attentive. This week, let's commit to creating quiet spaces where we can meet God. By embracing stillness and silencing distractions, we can tune in to His gentle whisper and experience the peace and guidance that comes from hearing His voice.

Closing Prayer

"Father, thank You for being a God who speaks to us in quiet moments. We are grateful for the ways You reveal Yourself in stillness and for the peace that Your presence brings. Help us to quiet our minds, remove distractions, and focus on You. As we go through this week, remind us to pause, be still, and listen for Your voice. May Your gentle whispers guide us, comfort us, and draw us closer to You. In Jesus' name, Amen."

Homework

Scripture Memory Verse:

Psalm 46:10 - *"Be still, and know that I am God; I will be exalted among the nations, I will be exalted in the earth."*

Daily Journal Reflection Topic:
Take a few minutes each day to sit in quietness, reflecting on God's presence. Write about any thoughts, feelings, or impressions that come during this time. Note how this stillness impacts your connection with God.

This session encourages participants to seek stillness and listen for God's voice, fostering a deeper awareness of His presence in quiet moments.

Notes:

Session 4: Seeing God's Work in Relationships

Opening Prayer

"Lord, thank You for the relationships You have blessed us with—our friends, family, mentors, and community. Help us to see Your presence in these connections and to recognize how You work through others to bring us love, support, and wisdom. Open our hearts to see how we can be vessels of Your love in the lives of those around us. May we grow in gratitude for the people in our lives and be encouraged to build relationships that reflect Your grace, kindness, and forgiveness. Guide our discussion today, and help us to draw closer to You and each other. In Jesus' name, we pray, Amen."

Session Introduction

Today's session focuses on seeing God's work in our relationships. God often uses the people around us to reveal His love, to encourage us, and to help us grow. These connections aren't random; they're a part of God's design to support and shape us in our faith journey. By learning to recognize God's presence in our interactions with others, we gain a greater appreciation for the people He has placed in our lives and how they reflect His character.

Reflection on Previous Week

Let's take a moment to reflect on last week's theme of hearing God's voice in quiet moments. Did you find moments of stillness where you felt closer to God? Was there a specific time you felt God's peace or guidance through silence? Share any insights or experiences from practicing stillness and listening for God's voice.

Reflection on Homework

The homework last week encouraged us to journal during quiet times. How did this practice of silence and reflection affect your week? Were there moments where you felt God speaking or nudging you through your thoughts? Reflecting on these quiet moments can deepen our awareness of His voice and help us see how He gently leads us.

Scripture Reading and Reflections

Proverbs 27:17

"As iron sharpens iron, so one person sharpens another."

Reflection:

This proverb reminds us that relationships refine and challenge us. God uses our interactions to shape us, encouraging growth, accountability, and wisdom. When we surround ourselves with people who support our faith, we can help each other grow spiritually and become stronger in our walk with God.

John 13:34-35

"A new command I give you: Love one another. As I have loved you, so you must love one another. By this everyone will know that you are my disciples, if you love one another."

Reflection:

Jesus calls us to love others as He loves us. This selfless, compassionate love is a reflection of God's own love for us. By practicing this love in our relationships, we reveal God's presence to the world. Our relationships become a testimony of God's love and the difference it makes in our lives.

Ecclesiastes 4:9-10

"Two are better than one, because they have a good return for their labor: If either of them falls down, one can help the other up. But pity anyone who falls and has no one to help them up."

Reflection:

This passage highlights the importance of companionship and support. God created us to live in community, where we can help and encourage each other. In relationships, we find strength, resilience, and comfort. Through these bonds, God provides us with support and guidance when we need it most.

1 Corinthians 13:4-7

"Love is patient, love is kind. It does not envy, it does not boast, it is not proud. It does not dishonor others, it is not self-seeking, it is not easily angered, it keeps no record of wrongs. Love does not delight in evil but rejoices with the truth. It always protects, always trusts, always hopes, always perseveres."

Reflection:

This passage beautifully describes the qualities of godly love. When we strive to embody these characteristics in our relationships, we reflect God's love to others. By being patient, kind, and forgiving, we allow God's love to shine through us, creating relationships that honor Him.

Discussion Points

In Proverbs 27:17, what does it mean for relationships to "sharpen" us? How have your relationships helped shape your faith?

Jesus commands us to love one another as He loves us. How can we show this selfless love in our daily interactions?

Ecclesiastes 4:9-10 speaks of the importance of companionship. When has someone in your life been a source of support during a difficult time?

In what ways can we be more intentional about building relationships that reflect the qualities described in 1 Corinthians 13?

How do our relationships with others reveal aspects of God's character?

Have you experienced a time when God used someone to encourage or challenge you in your faith? How did it impact you?

What are practical ways we can be vessels of God's love to those around us, even in small daily interactions?

How can recognizing God's presence in our relationships change the way we approach and value those connections?

Session Recap

Today, we explored how God works through our relationships. These connections are a powerful means through which God shapes, encourages, and supports us. By recognizing His presence in our relationships, we can better appreciate the people He has placed in our lives and learn to be vessels of His love for others. This week, let's focus on seeing each relationship as an opportunity to grow closer to God and to share His love.

Closing Prayer

"Father, thank You for the gift of relationships. We are grateful for the people You have placed in our lives to support, challenge, and love us. Help us to be aware of Your presence in our relationships and to see them as reflections of Your love. Teach us to show patience, kindness, and forgiveness, just as You show us. As we go through this week, guide us to be instruments of Your love and to appreciate the ways You work through the people around us. In Jesus' name, Amen."

Homework

Scripture Memory Verse:

John 13:34-35 - *"A new command I give you: Love one another. As I have loved you, so you must love one another. By this everyone will know that you are my disciples, if you love one another."*

Daily Journal Reflection Topic:
Each day, reflect on one interaction with another person and how God may have been present in that moment. Write down how that interaction reflects God's love, encouragement, or support.

This session encourages participants to recognize God's work in their relationships and to see each connection as an opportunity for spiritual growth and reflection of His love.

Notes:

Session 5: Discovering Purpose in Daily Tasks

Opening Prayer

"Dear Lord, thank You for the gift of each new day and the tasks You set before us. Often, we may overlook the purpose in our daily routines, but we know that You are present in every detail of our lives. Help us to see our work and responsibilities as opportunities to serve You and to bring You glory. Open our hearts and minds to understand that even in the ordinary, You are working to shape us and use us for Your purposes. Guide our time together today, and may we leave encouraged to approach each task with renewed purpose and joy. In Jesus' name, we pray, Amen."

Session Introduction

Today's session is about seeing purpose in the ordinary tasks we perform every day. From housework to job duties, these routines might sometimes feel mundane, but God uses them to shape us, strengthen us, and allow us to serve others. We'll explore how we can approach our daily work with a sense of purpose and intentionality, seeing each task as an offering to God. By shifting our perspective, we can recognize His presence in every aspect of our lives, even the small, repetitive actions.

Reflection on Previous Week

Let's take a moment to reflect on last week's theme of finding God's work in our relationships. How did focusing on God's presence in your connections with others impact your perspective? Did you experience moments of God working through someone in your life, or were you able to be a vessel of His love to someone else? Feel free to share any insights or meaningful experiences from the past week.

Reflection on Homework

The homework last week encouraged us to reflect on daily interactions and see how God was present. How did this practice affect your relationships and your awareness of God's role in them? Were there specific moments that stood out where you felt God's love working through others or through you? Reflecting on these experiences helps deepen our awareness of God's work in every connection.

Scripture Reading and Reflections

Colossians 3:23-24

"Whatever you do, work at it with all your heart, as working for the Lord, not for human masters, since you know that you will receive an inheritance from the Lord as a reward. It is the Lord Christ you are serving."

Reflection:

This passage encourages us to approach every task as though we're doing it for God, not just for human approval or personal gain. By putting our whole heart into our work, no matter how small or repetitive, we honor God and recognize that our effort serves a higher purpose. This verse invites us to see every task as an opportunity to bring glory to God.

1 Corinthians 10:31

"So whether you eat or drink or whatever you do, do it all for the glory of God."

Reflection:

Paul reminds us that even the most basic activities—eating and drinking—can be done for God's glory. This verse teaches us that no task is too small to offer up to God. By focusing on Him in everything we do, we give purpose to even the simplest actions, making them acts of worship.

Ecclesiastes 3:12-13

"I know that there is nothing better for people than to be happy and to do good while they live. That each of them may eat and drink and find satisfaction in all their toil—this is the gift of God."

Reflection:

This passage shows us that finding joy and satisfaction in our daily tasks is a gift from God. It encourages us to embrace our work, no matter how routine, with a positive spirit. God intends for us to find fulfillment in our efforts, reminding us that our work has value in His eyes.

Matthew 25:21

"His master replied, 'Well done, good and faithful servant! You have been faithful with a few things; I will put you in charge of many things. Come and share your master's happiness!'"

Reflection:

This verse highlights the importance of being faithful to the small responsibilities God gives us. By being diligent and trustworthy in our daily tasks, we honor God and prepare ourselves for greater opportunities in His service. This passage encourages us to approach our work with integrity and faithfulness, knowing that God values our efforts.

Discussion Points

In Colossians 3:23-24, how does working "with all your heart" for the Lord change the way we approach daily tasks?

How can we remember to bring glory to God, even in the smallest activities like eating and drinking, as mentioned in 1 Corinthians 10:31?

Ecclesiastes 3:12-13 talks about finding satisfaction in our work. What are some ways we can cultivate joy and gratitude in routine tasks?

How does Matthew 25:21 inspire us to be faithful in small responsibilities? Why do you think God values faithfulness in little things?

Can you think of a time when a seemingly mundane task became meaningful or purposeful for you? How did that affect your outlook on similar tasks?

What are some ways we can offer up our daily work as worship to God?

How does shifting our perspective on work and routine tasks help us see God's presence in every part of our lives?

What practical steps can we take this week to perform daily tasks with intentionality and purpose?

Session Recap

Today, we focused on discovering purpose in our daily tasks. We learned that every action, no matter how small, can be an offering to God when done with a willing heart and faithful spirit. By seeing our work as a way to honor God, we can find fulfillment and satisfaction in the routine. As we go through the coming week, let's remember that God is with us in every detail of our day, and each task is an opportunity to glorify Him.

Closing Prayer

"Lord, thank You for giving purpose to every part of our lives, even the simple tasks. Help us to approach each day with a heart willing to serve You, seeing each responsibility as an opportunity to bring You glory. Teach us to find joy in the work You have given us and to carry out each task faithfully. As we go through the week, may we remember that all we do is a reflection of our love for You. Guide us to honor You in every moment, and may our actions reflect Your goodness. In Jesus' name, Amen."

Homework

Scripture Memory Verse:

Colossians 3:23-24 - *"Whatever you do, work at it with all your heart, as working for the Lord, not for human masters, since you know that you will receive an inheritance from the Lord as a reward. It is the Lord Christ you are serving."*

Daily Journal Reflection Topic:

Reflect each day on one task that you often find mundane or repetitive. Write about how approaching it as an offering to God changes your attitude or brings a new sense of purpose.

This session encourages participants to approach their daily tasks with intentionality, seeing them as opportunities to honor God.

Notes:

Session 6: Recognizing God's Guidance in Challenges

Opening Prayer

"Heavenly Father, we thank You for Your guidance in all aspects of our lives, especially during challenging times. Often, we may struggle to see Your hand at work when we face difficulties, but we trust that You are with us, guiding and strengthening us. Help us to see challenges as opportunities to grow closer to You, to deepen our faith, and to recognize Your presence. Open our hearts today to hear Your voice and to see Your loving guidance, even in the midst of trials. In Jesus' name, we pray, Amen."

Session Introduction

Today's session focuses on seeing God's presence and guidance in our challenges. Life can be difficult, and it's natural to feel overwhelmed at times. But God promises to be with us, especially during hard times, and to use those moments to strengthen us, teach us, and shape us. This session will help us explore how we can turn to God in our struggles, trust in His plan, and find purpose in our challenges.

Reflection on Previous Week

Let's reflect on last week's theme of finding purpose in daily tasks. How did focusing on God's presence in your routines impact your perspective? Did you experience moments of peace or joy in tasks that often feel mundane? Feel free to share any insights or transformations you noticed throughout the week.

Reflection on Homework

The homework last week asked us to choose one task each day and reflect on it as an offering to God. How did this practice affect your approach to your responsibilities? Did you feel a shift in how you viewed even the smallest tasks? Reflecting on these experiences helps us build habits of gratitude and purpose.

Scripture Reading and Reflections

James 1:2-4

"Consider it pure joy, my brothers and sisters, whenever you face trials of many kinds, because you know that the testing of your faith produces perseverance. Let perseverance finish its work so that you may be mature and complete, not lacking anything."

Reflection:

This passage encourages us to view challenges as opportunities for growth. While difficulties may be painful, they strengthen our faith and help us develop perseverance. God uses challenges to mold us, making us more mature and complete in our walk with Him. This verse invites us to trust that God has a purpose for every trial.

Romans 8:28

"And we know that in all things God works for the good of those who love him, who have been called according to his purpose."

Reflection:

This verse reminds us that God is always at work, even in our hardships. While we may not understand His plan, we can trust that He is using each situation for our good and His glory. This passage reassures us that nothing in our lives is outside of God's control, and He is able to turn every situation into something beneficial for our growth.

2 Corinthians 12:9-10

"But he said to me, 'My grace is sufficient for you, for my power is made perfect in weakness.' Therefore I will boast all the more gladly about my weaknesses, so that Christ's power may rest on me. That is why, for Christ's sake, I delight in weaknesses, in insults, in hardships, in persecutions, in difficulties. For when I am weak, then I am strong."

Reflection:

Paul's words remind us that God's strength is most evident in our weaknesses. Our challenges give God an opportunity to show His power and grace in our lives. When we acknowledge our own limitations, we invite God's strength to work through us. This passage encourages us to lean on God and trust that His grace is sufficient for every trial.

Psalm 34:17-18

"The righteous cry out, and the Lord hears them; he delivers them from all their troubles. The Lord is close to the brokenhearted and saves those who are crushed in spirit."

Reflection:

This psalm reassures us of God's nearness during our darkest moments. When we feel broken or overwhelmed, God is especially close, offering comfort and deliverance. This verse is a reminder that God is compassionate and attentive to our struggles, and we can rely on His presence and care when we need it most.

Discussion Points

James 1:2-4 encourages us to "consider it pure joy" when we face trials. How can we shift our perspective to see challenges as opportunities for growth?

In what ways has a past struggle strengthened your faith or deepened your relationship with God?

Romans 8:28 speaks of God working all things for our good. How can we hold onto this promise when we face difficult or confusing situations?

How does acknowledging our weaknesses, as Paul did in 2 Corinthians 12:9-10, allow us to experience God's strength?

How can we develop a habit of turning to God for guidance when we first encounter a problem rather than trying to handle it alone?

Psalm 34:17-18 speaks of God's closeness to the brokenhearted. How does this verse bring comfort during hard times?

How can we remind ourselves that God has a purpose for our trials, even if we don't see the outcome right away?

What are some practical ways we can support each other in our challenges, helping one another to rely on God's guidance and strength?

Session Recap

In today's session, we discussed recognizing God's guidance in challenges. We learned that God uses difficulties to strengthen our faith, draw us closer to Him, and reveal His power and grace. As we go through trials, we can trust that God is with us, guiding us, and working for our good. This week, let's try to see each struggle as an opportunity to grow closer to God and to experience His loving guidance.

Closing Prayer

"Lord, thank You for being with us in every trial and hardship. Thank You for using challenges to shape us, strengthen us, and draw us closer to You. Help us to see our struggles as opportunities to rely on Your strength and to grow in faith. Remind us of Your promises and Your constant presence, even when things feel overwhelming. Guide us this week to trust in Your plan, to lean on Your grace, and to seek You in all circumstances. In Jesus' name, Amen."

Homework

Scripture Memory Verse:

Romans 8:28 - *"And we know that in all things God works for the good of those who love him, who have been called according to his purpose."*

Daily Journal Reflection Topic:

Each day, reflect on a challenge or difficult moment you faced.

Write about how God might be using this experience for your growth and how you can trust Him more deeply through it.

This session encourages participants to see challenges as opportunities to rely on God, trusting that He is working through every trial.

**Notes:

Session 7:
Celebrating Everyday Joys

Opening Prayer

"Gracious Lord, thank You for the countless blessings You give us each day. Often, we overlook the small joys You place in our lives, but today we come with grateful hearts, ready to see and celebrate them. Open our eyes to recognize Your gifts, and help us to cultivate a spirit of gratitude. May we experience joy in the simple things, knowing that each blessing is a reminder of Your love and presence. Guide us in our time together, and let us leave with hearts full of thanksgiving. In Jesus' name, we pray, Amen."

Session Introduction

In today's session, we're focusing on celebrating the everyday joys that God provides. Life can be busy, and it's easy to overlook the small, beautiful moments that make each day special. But God delights in blessing us, and when we take time to notice these little joys, our hearts grow more grateful and aware of His goodness. This session will encourage us to slow down, recognize God's gifts, and cultivate a lifestyle of gratitude and joy.

Reflection on Previous Week

Let's reflect on last week's theme of recognizing God's guidance in challenges. Did focusing on God's presence during difficult moments help you gain new strength or perspective? Were you able to see ways that God might be using those challenges for growth? Feel free to share any insights or experiences that stood out.

Reflection on Homework

The homework last week asked us to reflect on a daily challenge and consider how God might be working through it. How did this practice impact your perspective? Did you find that reflecting on God's purpose in your challenges helped you approach them with more faith or patience? This exercise helps us build resilience and trust in God's plan for our lives.

Scripture Reading and Reflections

Philippians 4:4-7

"Rejoice in the Lord always. I will say it again: Rejoice! Let your gentleness be evident to all. The Lord is near. Do not be anxious about anything, but in every situation, by prayer and petition, with thanksgiving, present your requests to God. And the peace of God, which transcends all understanding, will guard your hearts and your minds in Christ Jesus."

Reflection:

Paul encourages us to rejoice always, regardless of circumstances, and to cultivate a heart of gratitude. By focusing on God's nearness and bringing our concerns to Him, we can experience His peace. This passage reminds us that joy isn't dependent on external situations but on our relationship with God.

Psalm 118:24

"This is the day that the Lord has made; let us rejoice and be glad in it."

Reflection:

Each day is a gift from God, an opportunity to rejoice in His goodness and grace. This verse encourages us to start each day with gratitude and to seek joy in the blessings that God provides. By recognizing each day as a new gift, we can approach life with a sense of wonder and appreciation.

John 15:11

"I have told you this so that my joy may be in you and that your joy may be complete."

Reflection:

Jesus promises us His own joy, a joy that is deep and lasting. This joy isn't based on temporary circumstances but is a gift that comes from knowing Him. This verse reminds us that true joy is found in a close relationship with Christ, who fills our lives with purpose and meaning.

1 Thessalonians 5:16-18

"Rejoice always, pray continually, give thanks in all circumstances; for this is God's will for you in Christ Jesus."

Reflection:

Paul's instructions are clear: we're called to rejoice, pray, and give thanks in every circumstance. This doesn't mean ignoring hardships but finding reasons to be grateful even in difficult times. Cultivating gratitude and joy helps us stay close to God and align our hearts with His will.

Discussion Points

Philippians 4:4-7 calls us to rejoice always. How can we maintain a joyful heart even when things aren't going well?

Psalm 118:24 encourages us to see each day as a gift. How can starting our day with this mindset affect our outlook?

Jesus speaks of giving us His joy in John 15:11. What do you think it means to have Christ's joy within us, and how does it differ from worldly happiness?

1 Thessalonians 5:16-18 instructs us to give thanks in all circumstances. What are some ways we can find gratitude during difficult or mundane moments?

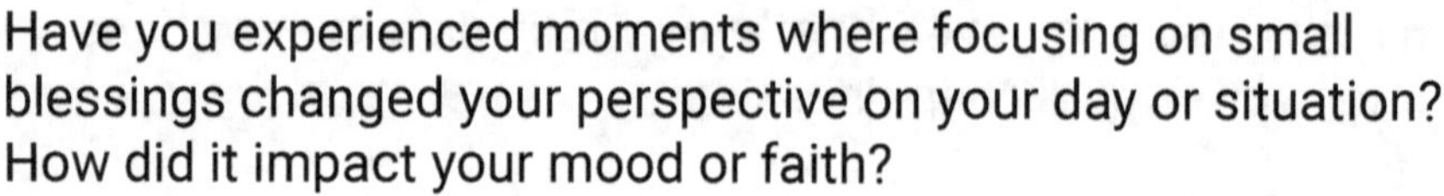

Have you experienced moments where focusing on small blessings changed your perspective on your day or situation? How did it impact your mood or faith?

What are some practical steps we can take to remind ourselves to notice and celebrate everyday joys?

How can we share our joy and gratitude with others, and why is this important in our faith journey?

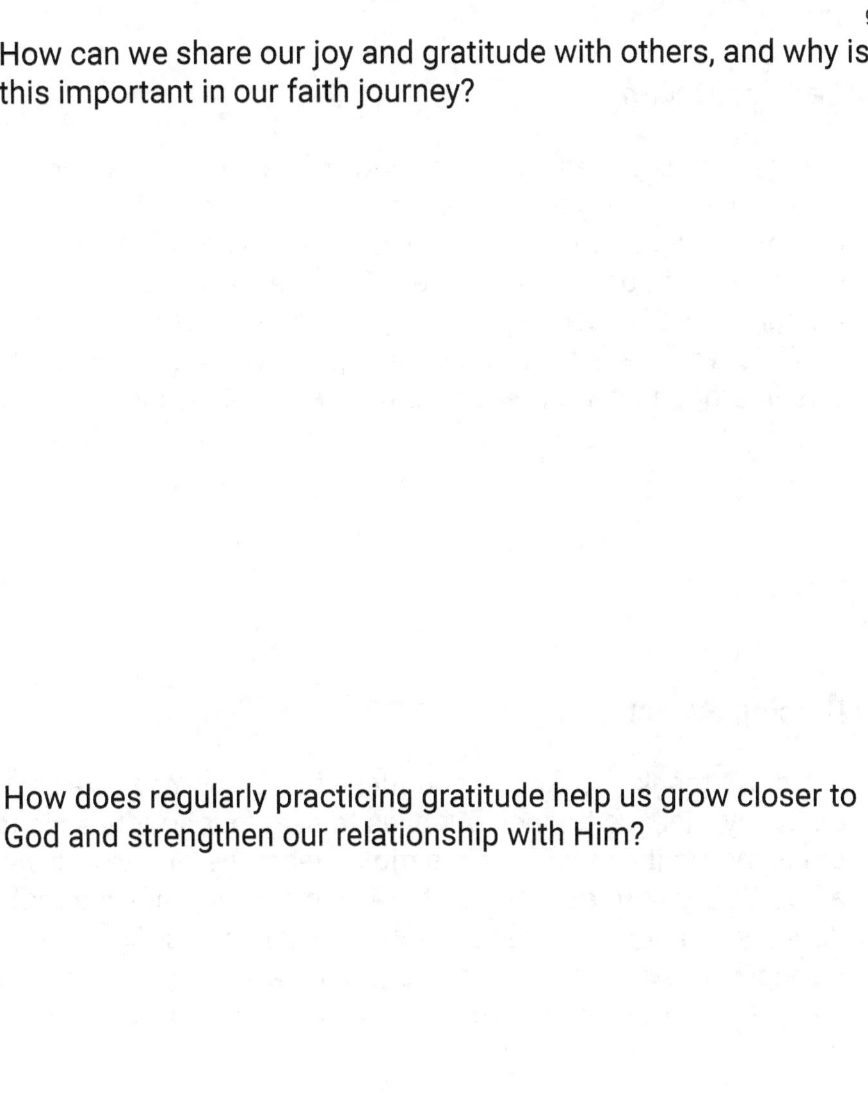

How does regularly practicing gratitude help us grow closer to God and strengthen our relationship with Him?

Session Recap

Today, we discussed the importance of celebrating everyday joys and cultivating a heart of gratitude. By taking time to notice God's blessings, we can experience His peace and joy, regardless of our circumstances. Each day is an opportunity to recognize His presence and to rejoice in the gifts He has given us. This week, let's focus on finding joy in the small things, trusting that each moment of gratitude brings us closer to God.

Closing Prayer

"Lord, we thank You for the countless blessings You give us each day. Help us to open our eyes to see Your goodness in the small moments, to find joy in simple pleasures, and to cultivate a heart of gratitude. Teach us to rejoice always, knowing that Your joy is a gift that strengthens and sustains us. As we go through this week, may we celebrate the everyday joys You provide, and may our hearts overflow with thanksgiving. In Jesus' name, Amen."

Homework

- **Scripture Memory Verse:**
  Psalm 118:24 - *"This is the day that the Lord has made; let us rejoice and be glad in it."*
- **Daily Journal Reflection Topic:**
  Each day, write about one small moment or blessing that brought you joy. Reflect on how this moment reminds you of God's presence and love.

This session encourages participants to celebrate small joys and cultivate gratitude as a way to experience God's peace and joy more fully.

Notes:

Session 8: Reflecting on the Journey and Moving Forward

Opening Prayer

"Dear Lord, thank You for guiding us through this journey of learning to see Your presence in the small and beautiful moments of life. We have grown in our understanding of Your love, Your grace, and Your joy that fills our everyday lives. As we reflect on the past sessions, help us to hold onto the lessons You have shown us. Let these truths remain in our hearts as we move forward, allowing us to live each day more fully aware of You. Guide our hearts today as we look back on what we've learned and as we look forward to how we will continue to grow. In Jesus' name, Amen."

Session Introduction

Today's session is a time of reflection and celebration. Over the past weeks, we've explored how to see God's work in various aspects of life—from nature to relationships, from challenges to simple joys. This session is an opportunity to review what we've learned, celebrate our growth, and commit to carrying these practices forward. By integrating these lessons into our lives, we can continue to grow closer to God and live each day with a renewed sense of awareness of His presence.

Reflection on the Journey

Let's take some time to reflect on the journey we've taken together over these past sessions. We started by learning to open our eyes to God's presence in everyday life. We went on to see Him in nature, hear His voice in quiet moments, and feel His love in our relationships. We also learned to find purpose in our daily tasks, recognize His guidance in challenges, and celebrate everyday joys. As we think about these themes, consider which moments or insights have impacted you the most and how you have felt God working in your life through this study.

Reflection on Homework

Throughout the study, we have practiced journaling, reflecting, and noticing God's presence in different areas of our lives. Reflect on how these practices have influenced your faith journey. Has journaling helped you recognize more of God's presence? Have you noticed any changes in your mindset or daily habits that have drawn you closer to God?

Scripture Reading and Reflections

Philippians 1:6

"Being confident of this, that he who began a good work in you will carry it on to completion until the day of Christ Jesus."

Reflection: This verse reminds us that our spiritual journey is ongoing. God has started a good work within us, and He is faithful to continue and complete it. As we move forward, we can be confident that He will keep guiding us and helping us grow.

Lamentations 3:22-23

"Because of the Lord's great love we are not consumed, for his compassions never fail. They are new every morning; great is your faithfulness."

Reflection: Each day is a fresh start, filled with God's mercy and faithfulness. As we carry the lessons of this study into our daily lives, we can trust that God's love and compassion will meet us anew every morning, encouraging us to seek Him continually.

Psalm 139:23-24

"Search me, God, and know my heart; test me and know my anxious thoughts. See if there is any offensive way in me, and lead me in the way everlasting."

Reflection: This psalm invites God to search our hearts and lead us in His ways. As we reflect on what we've learned, this verse encourages us to remain open to God's guidance and to allow Him to shape and direct us.

Isaiah 43:19

"See, I am doing a new thing! Now it springs up; do you not perceive it? I am making a way in the wilderness and streams in the wasteland."

Reflection: God is always at work, creating new paths and possibilities for us. This verse is a beautiful reminder that He is continually doing new things in our lives, making ways where there seems to be none. As we move forward, we can trust that God will continue to guide us into new blessings and opportunities.

Discussion Points

Philippians 1:6 speaks of God's promise to complete the work He began in us. How does this encourage you as you continue your faith journey?

How can we remind ourselves each morning, as Lamentations 3:22-23 suggests, that God's mercies are new and available to us?

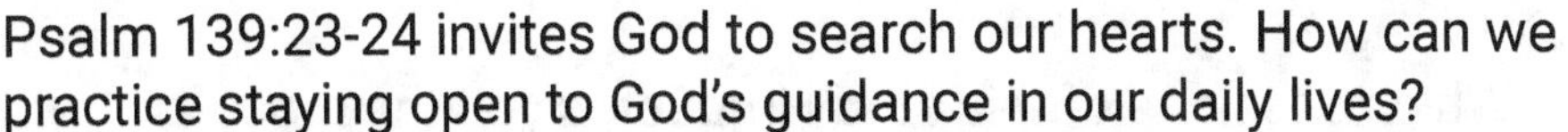

Psalm 139:23-24 invites God to search our hearts. How can we practice staying open to God's guidance in our daily lives?

Isaiah 43:19 encourages us to see God doing new things. How can we remain receptive to God's ongoing work in our lives, especially when we feel stuck?

Which sessions of this study impacted you the most, and why?

What changes have you noticed in your daily habits or mindset as a result of this study?

How can we encourage one another to keep noticing God's presence in our everyday lives?

What are some ways you plan to incorporate what you've learned into your ongoing spiritual journey?

Session Recap

Today, we celebrated the journey we've taken together in learning to see God's presence in everyday life. From recognizing Him in nature to finding joy in daily moments, we've grown in awareness and gratitude. As we move forward, let's carry these lessons with us, confident that God will continue to reveal Himself in new ways. Each day brings fresh opportunities to experience His love, guidance, and joy. May we commit to a life of attentiveness, looking for the small miracles He places in our path.

Closing Prayer

"Father, thank You for guiding us through this journey. Thank You for each lesson, each blessing, and each moment where we've felt Your presence. As we move forward, help us to carry these truths with us, keeping our hearts open to see You in every detail of life. May we be filled with gratitude, joy, and a desire to know You more each day. Guide us to walk closely with You, trusting that You will complete the good work You have begun in us. In Jesus' name, we pray, Amen."

Homework

- **Scripture Memory Verse:**
  Philippians 1:6 - *"Being confident of this, that he who began a good work in you will carry it on to completion until the day of Christ Jesus."*
- **Daily Journal Reflection Topic:**
  Reflect each day on how God has worked in your life throughout this study. Write down one thing you are grateful for and one way you hope to continue seeing His presence in your daily life.

This final session encourages participants to celebrate their journey and commit to ongoing growth and awareness of God's presence.

Notes: